The Gentle **GIANT**

Tom McClure—A Journey of Commitment and Obedience to God

Pat McClure

purposeful design.
p u b l i c a t i o n s
A Division of ACSI

Colorado Springs, CO

© 2007 by Pat McClure
Published by ACSI/Purposeful Design Publications

Purposeful Design Publications is the publishing division of the Association of Christian Schools International (ACSI) and is committed to the ministry of Christian school education, to enable Christian educators and schools worldwide to effectively prepare students for life. As the publisher of textbooks, trade books, and other educational resources within ACSI, Purposeful Design Publications strives to produce biblically sound materials that reflect Christian scholarship and stewardship and that address the identified needs of Christian schools around the world.

Unless otherwise identified, all Scripture quotations are taken from the Holy Bible, New International Version® (NIV®), © 1973, 1978, 1984 by International Bible Society. All rights reserved worldwide. The "NIV" and "New International Version" are trademarks registered in the United States Patent and Trademark Office by International Bible Society. Use of either trademark requires the permission of International Bible Society.

Printed in the United States of America
16 15 14 13 12 11 10 09 08 07   1 2 3 4 5 6 7

McClure, Pat
      The gentle giant: Tom McClure—a journey of commitment and obedience to God
      ISBN 978-1-58331-088-5 Catalog #6589
Designer: Megan Morales
Editorial team: Mary Endres, Karen Friesen

Purposeful Design Publications
A Division of ACSI
PO Box 65130 • Colorado Springs, CO 80962-5130
Customer Service: 800-367-0798 • Website: www.acsi.org

DEDICATED TO

The memory of Tom McClure—
A devoted family man,
A respected educator, and
A courageous missionary
Who loved God with all his
Heart, soul, and mind

Our loving children—
Stephanie and Dan Bishop,
Clayton and Heidi McClure

Our precious grandchildren—
Haley, Jonathan Thomas, Ethan, Micah, and Jonah

Our entire supportive ACSI family and
The terrific ACSI Europe staff—
Alan, Malinda, Laci, Anna, Ervin, Helen,
Priscilla, Daniel, and Felicia

The caring Janz Team Ministries—
Jack, Lois, Janet, Gary, and
The whole group.

Contents

Foreword   7

A Note to the Reader   9

Acknowledgments   11

Special Thanks   13

Chapter 1: A Private Faith   15

Chapter 2: It All Started with a Prank   19

Chapter 3: The Bear Story   23

Chapter 4: Weeping Father   27

Chapter 5: Encourager   31

Chapter 6: Obedient Servant   35

Chapter 7: Dedicated Educator   39

Chapter 8: Missionary Heart   45

Chapter 9: Called to Missions   51

Chapter 10: The Missionary   55

Chapter 11: Courageous Hero   63

Personal Testimony: Thomas A. McClure   69

Tom McClure International Teacher Awards   71

FOREWORD

As I read through this brief account of the life of my friend Tom, I was reminded of the gentle giant of a man that Tom was as he lived and walked among us.

Tom and I came into the Association of Christian Schools International (ACSI) at about the same time. As I came to know Tom, I came to know a man who had a sensitivity to God that I have found in only a few. My area of responsibility in ACSI took me all over the world, and as Tom and I would have time for fellowship at staff meetings or during an ACSI convention, Tom would always want to know what God was doing around the world in Christian schooling. When I shared with him, he would often tell me that he was praying that he and his wife, Pat, could serve God overseas as missionaries. Tom was passionate about sharing his love for Jesus.

I knew Tom as a man of deep commitment both to his Lord Jesus and to his family. He walked the journey of life with a dedicated obedience to the call of God, willing to go where God called him regardless of the cost.

Tom had been deeply touched and compelled by ministering through the CoMission as he helped take Christ to Russian public school teachers. God used this experience and other cross-cultural ministry experiences of Tom's as a catalyst to fulfill His call on Tom's life to serve as a missionary educator. At age 60, Tom sacrificed much as he obeyed Christ's call to serve in a cross-cultural ministry in Hungary.

Tom was so excited that God was using him to touch the nations. As a testimony to Tom's unwavering commitment, I draw a quote from this book that demonstrates his obedience to his Master. Following the accident that ultimately took Tom's life, Tom remarked, "If I had known before we left for Hungary that I would soon die, I would have gone anyway." Tom's words are a bit reminiscent of a quote from Jim Elliot, a missionary martyr in Ecuador: "He is no fool who gives up what he cannot keep to gain what he cannot lose." Tom was a man of humility, reflecting the heart of Jesus, who did not come to be served but to serve and to give His life.

I hope you will be challenged to a greater depth of personal commitment as you read this book and reflect on the life of my friend Tom and his love for the Savior.

Philip Renicks, EdD
Vice President, International Ministries
ACSI
June 2007

A Note to the Reader

It is a rare privilege to encounter someone whose life touches thousands around the world. Tom was such a man. His life of commitment to God has left a legacy for generations. As you read this book, may your heart be encouraged to live a life of dedication and obedience to God, whatever God calls you to do and wherever He calls you to go. May you always begin each day and each prayer as Tom did:

"I love you, Jesus."

This book is my gift to you from Tom.

ACKNOWLEDGMENTS

I would like to express a special note of thanks to my friends and family for all the love and care you have shown to me. Your prayers have kept me strong. Thank you, and God bless each of you.

I would especially like to thank my children and grandchildren, who have loved me through my healing time. And special thanks to my sisters, Barbara and Michele; my brother, Bill; and other friends who kept encouraging me to write and complete this book. ACSI and Steve Babbitt, director of publications, deserve a great big thanks for their support and for choosing to publish this book. Thank you to ACSI editors for making the manuscript readable. Thank you, Martha Phyllis, for your willingness to read, to correct, and to give me structural advice and encouragement. Thank you, Terry Hash, who had faith that this book would be a healing tool for me as well as a legacy for Tom.

SPECIAL THANKS

To ...

The compassionate staff of Kecskemet Hospital, Hungary

The dedicated staff of Shepherd Center

The tender care at Henry Medical Center

The loving care at Southern Crescent Acute Care Facility

The comforting care at Christian Ministries Hospice

CHAPTER 1

A PRIVATE FAITH

Jesus, it is all about you! It is not about me. I truly love you, Jesus. Even as I lie here paralyzed from the shoulders down, knowing that I am slowly dying, I will always love you, Jesus. I look at the machines that surround me—the ventilator, the oxygen machine, the machine that registers my pulse and breathing—there is a constant beeping or humming. Otherwise, it is quiet. No one else is in my room. Oh, Lord, when will you take me home to be with you? I am so ready, and I've told my family I'm ready—soon, Lord, soon.

The techs have just finished with my bed bath. I went into another choking spasm as they rolled me back and forth, back and forth. Is this the way I'm going to die? Will I choke to death? Father, I pray that I will not die this way. Finally, the choking has stopped, and I am breathing better. Every day I dread my bath, since it always makes me choke and struggle to breathe. How long have I been here in this hospice center? The days run together. If Pat hadn't put up a wall board on which she writes each day and month, I wouldn't know what day or month it is.

Is it time for Pat to come? I can't wait for her to come even though I can't communicate with her anymore. Somehow she knows I hear her even though I don't respond. I'm glad she still talks and reads to me; I love to hear her voice and see her face.

It must be close to Christmas. Pat put up a tree and a garland, so my room looks festive. Pat knows how much I love Christmastime— decorating, making candy, being with my family—and sharing the love of Christ as He came down at Christmas. Christ knew from the beginning that He was born to suffer and die, but He still came. Lord, as I lie here and suffer, may I be thankful that you've allowed me to share in your suffering. I long to be with you in heaven. I'll miss Pat and my family, but I'm eager to meet you in my heavenly home and to suffer no more.

Pat has finally arrived. She's turned on some beautiful, soothing hymns that minister to my heart. I look forward to her coming into my room each morning. She always says she loves me. Then she reads a devotional, prays with me, reads cards and emails that have come, and caresses my face and hair. Usually she gives me a shave whether I really need it or not. I love her touching my face and talking to me, even though I can't talk back. I pray that she will never stop talking to me though I know it seems to her that I don't hear her. In the quietness of this morning, I ask myself, "How did I come to this place in such a short time? Lord, what purpose has all this served in your kingdom? Will I ever know the 'why' in this lifetime?" As I ponder these questions and think about my life, I wonder, "Have I been an obedient servant to my Lord and Savior?" My mind begins to drift and drift to an earlier time—a much earlier time.

I remember when I was an eight-year-old boy, and the Sunday school teacher shared with me how to be saved. I wanted to be saved, so she prayed with me. I believe I gave Jesus all I knew how to give at that time. But no one ever discipled me and helped me grow in my walk with the Lord. Therefore, I was bombarded for many years with doubts about my salvation. It wasn't until much later, when I was in Atlanta and working for ACSI, that I finally settled the issue once and for all, made a public profession of my faith, and was baptized a second time. I have never doubted again.

It seems strange to think about that young boy so full of life and wonder, with a whole life ahead of him. Who would have thought at that time that this boy would someday be paralyzed and dying? Life takes unusual turns as we walk the path with Christ. Even then Christ knew what would happen to me and had begun to prepare me for the suffering that lay ahead.

I was privileged to be raised in a Christian home with loving and caring parents who also loved the Lord. They were thrilled when I was saved as a young boy, but as I grew I never understood the importance of sharing my faith and living it out in front of others. My parents considered their faith very private, and I was not taught how to witness to others about Christ. I am sad that I missed out on so many years when I could have been a witness for the Lord. Maybe that is why I have such a fervor to witness now.

I see that boy becoming a high school athlete who played many sports and was gifted at them. I also cared about my classmates and was always a kind, gentle guy. In fact, I was nicknamed the "Gentle Giant." But I hurt inside because I never shared with my classmates the most important aspect of my life, my Savior, Jesus Christ. I remember times when I wanted to tell everyone about my precious Lord, but my pride stood in the way. What would they think of me? Now I wish I had told them and hadn't cared what they thought. I can't go back. But I think it is because I failed to witness then that I became a bold witness later, even more so now as I come to the end of my life.

Now I see a college freshman with a football scholarship. Supposedly, I had the world by the tail! But once I got to college, I found out that I wasn't the only one with talent on the field. My eyes were truly opened, and my pride fell by the wayside. I see now that this experience was good, as it put into perspective my own picture of myself. I know that the Lord was working on me, even then—shaping me into a humble and kind and caring person. There is no doubt in my mind that pride could have been an issue for me because I played college ball. But God kept my feet on the ground—mostly by means of the hits and tackles I took. I was one sore guy after the first couple of weeks of practice. I don't think there was a place on my body that did not have a bump or bruise or cut. I kept telling myself that this was going to be fun—eventually. I found out very quickly that college ball is quite different from high school ball. But I hung in there and made the freshman traveling team, which was quite a feat, as most of the freshmen were cut or gave up and went home. I must have been blind, for I wasn't seeing God in all of these events. But He was working in my life. Soon I would meet my lifelong mate, and God was at work in that as well.

CHAPTER 2

IT ALL STARTED WITH A PRANK

I see Pat reading a book. Every now and then she glances over at me and smiles. I try to smile back, but it doesn't happen. I think she knows I see her. Wait, now she's getting up and coming over. She's talking to me about some funny thing that happened with the grandchildren, and all the while she is stroking my head and looking down and smiling at me. I hope she knows I hear her. I love it when she's close to me and touching my head and face; it makes me feel very close to her. I remember back when we first met. It was a funny event, but eventually it led to our dating and falling in love. Let's see if I can remember, remember ...

───────◆───────

It was early in the winter quarter at college, and football season was over. Since I wasn't playing football then, as an athlete I had to do jobs around the campus on Saturday to earn my scholarship. One of my jobs was waxing and buffing the halls in the girls' dorm. That day I was cleaning the dorm hallway of a girl I was dating. One of the strict rules of that day was that guys could not go into a girl's room at any time. So I was just leaning inside the doorway of her room, and she was giving me cookies to munch on. Well, some of the girls played a trick on me. They got Pat to act as the floor advisor and chew me out for standing in the doorway. She put on a good act, and I thought I was in *big* trouble until all the girls started laughing, including Pat. I had never met Pat, but I was not happy with the joke. I gave her an "I'll get you" look.

I found out which room was hers, and on the next several Saturday mornings, bright and early, I banged the huge buffing machine against her door to wake her up. Her roommate was not pleased, and neither was Pat. Actually, I thought the prank was quite inventive. After doing the same thing several Saturdays in a row, I gave her a break. I felt I had settled the issue. I didn't know that our paths would cross again in a few weeks.

Pat and I had the same required science class. It was in one of those huge theater-style classrooms with a hundred plus students in it. The professor stood way at the bottom of the classroom, so we could hardly see him. We were seated alphabetically, and since Pat's last name started with L, and mine with M, I was a few rows behind her. I'd recognized her as the "trickster" from the dorm event, so I decided to get even. I had a group of my buddies sitting close by, so this was really going to be fun. Before class, as she turned around to talk with a friend behind her, she glanced in my direction, and I gave her a huge wink—you know, one of those winks that is overplayed. She turned the brightest shade of red I'd ever seen, and the guys and I had a good laugh. She was embarrassed and quickly turned back around. The next day, for some reason she looked in my direction again, and of course I winked again. Again, she turned bright red, and this time she looked a little angry. The guys and I laughed again, but I was beginning to feel badly. I was afraid I'd hurt her feelings, so it wasn't funny any more.

Afterward, I ran to catch up with her as she hurried to her next class. She turned around and saw me coming, so she speeded up, hoping to lose me. I caught up with her and apologized over and over for embarrassing her. I said it had started as a joke. I told her I knew that I'd hurt her feelings, and I didn't want to do that. She stopped, looked up at me, and smiled. She said it was okay, but please don't do it again. She added that she hates the way she blushes so easily, and sometimes it gets embarrassing. I told her I thought it was cute and I wouldn't bug her again. I continued walking with her as we made our way to our next classes—actually it was nowhere near my next class, but I was enjoying the company. We talked and laughed about nothing, and I found myself drawn to her.

As we reached her next class, I blurted out that I had an intramural basketball game that night and would she like to come by and watch. She said she'd think about it, as she had lots of work to prepare for tomorrow's classes. I said goodbye, told her I hoped to see her that night, and ran to my next class.

Well, she showed up for the game. I was very pleased and wanted to put on a show of how good I was. I think I made more blunders in that game than any I'd ever played. After the game, I walked her back to the dorm, and we talked and talked. She was easy to talk with, and I felt comfortable with her. We talked about where we came from, our families, our high school years, and on and on. Once we got to the dorm, we stood outside and talked some more. Finally, I asked her out. There was a college wrestling match that Friday night, and I asked her to go with me. She said she knew absolutely nothing about wrestling, but I promised to educate her during the match. Nodding her head yes, she agreed to go with me, and then off she went to her room. I was eager for Friday night. I didn't have a car, so we'd have to walk from the dorm to the gym, but that would be fun.

As we had talked, I found out what classes she had, and I showed up the next day to walk with her after one of them. She had a break and so did I, so we went to the student union, got a Coke, and talked some more. She was fun to be with, and she laughed at my jokes, funny or not. She said she loved my sense of humor and the way I made her laugh. I was at ease with her, and I felt a certain attraction to her from the start. I reminded her about the dorm prank, and we laughed about that. I told her I thought it was a neat trick and she'd carried it off very well. We laughed some more. I really enjoyed being with her and looked forward to our times together. The rest of the week, I met her several times after class, and we would walk and talk and laugh. She was fun, and I loved being with her.

We had a great time at the wrestling match, but she said that she felt so dumb not knowing anything about what we were seeing. I spent most of the time telling her what was going on and had fun introducing her to wrestling. That was the first of many dates, and our affection for each other grew and grew. I knew that I would have to talk with her about whether she was a Christian. I didn't think she was as she never talked about it, but actually I didn't either. I knew that I ought to date only a Christian, but she was so good and wholesome that I thought surely she was a Christian.

After many dates, I got brave and shared with her about my faith in Jesus. She had a rather puzzled look on her face, so I explained it again. Then she said yes, she believed that Jesus was the Son of God and that He died on the cross. I thought she must be a Christian, and I was relieved. But deep in my heart, I wasn't sure she really understood what it meant to be a Christian—to be born again and have a personal relationship with Jesus. But this was a start—at least she says she's a Christian.

I took her to meet my parents. They shared their faith with her as well, and she still said she was a Christian. Who was I to question or to judge? I met her grandparents, as her parents were in another state where her dad was stationed. Her father was in the Air Force, and she had traveled all over the world. I had barely been out of Colorado. Her grandparents were wonderful Christians, and we hit it off right away. I didn't have any living grandparents, so it was so neat to be with them.

The rest of the school year, we were together as often as we could be. I was falling in love, and so was she. We were just right for each other—like two puzzle pieces fitting together perfectly. Her weak points were my strong points, and vice versa. I wanted to marry her, but her dad was against our making any commitment until after graduation—and that was a long time away. We continued to talk about marriage, but always in the future.

That summer she went back to Virginia to be with her family. I stayed in Colorado and worked, and I secretly saved money to buy her a ring. I wanted to surprise her in the fall when she came back to school. I thought that if we got engaged maybe her father would give in and we could marry sooner. I had big plans and big ideas.

CHAPTER 3

THE BEAR STORY

Oh, here comes the nurse to give me my tube feeding. They joke about it being a milkshake; I wish it were, and I wish I could taste it. The nurses and techs here are kind and compassionate. They always talk to me as they are working with me, as if I can hear and understand. That makes me feel a little more like a human, not just a body lying totally still. I would love to have a big hamburger and a Coke, but I know that's impossible. Actually, I can almost taste them. I guess that's a taste you never forget. Well, she's finished, and I didn't taste a thing after all. Now, back to what I was remembering ... college, summer ... oh yes, the bear story. That's a good one!

———◆———

The summer when Pat was in Virginia and I was in Colorado seemed long and drawn out. I missed being with her, but I busied myself with work and hanging out with some of my old high school buddies. One day we saw a promotion at a local shopping center about wrestling a bear. A person actually had to pay to wrestle a bear, and if he could stay in the ring (just a tarp over the asphalt) with the bear for three minutes, he'd win a prize of a hundred dollars. But who in his right mind would think he could wrestle a bear for three minutes?

Believe it or not, the guys talked me into wrestling that bear. Actually the bear didn't look too big standing on all fours. Besides, he was declawed and muzzled.

Anyway, the guys paid the dollar for me to wrestle. I was in my corner bending up and down, getting ready for contact, when the bell rang. I turned around and faced the bear, now standing on his hind legs. He was *huge!* The bear pulled me into his chest and gave me a genuine "bear hug." The smell was horrible, and I thought I'd suffocate. Finally, I was able to push away from the bear, and I tripped him up with my leg, swiping his legs out from under him. He fell on his back. Aha! I had him. I ran and jumped right into the middle of his belly, hoping I could keep him down. But somehow the bear got his back feet under me and with one move sent me flying across the ring. I landed with a loud *thud*!

I was dazed, but the bear kept coming at me and continued to wrestle, putting me into actual wrestling holds, and each time I would work my way out. Finally, I was exhausted, and I crawled out of the ring short of the three-minute mark and the prize. My heart was beating so hard and fast that I thought it was coming out of my chest. I was gasping for air, and I really smelled.

The bear crawled off, sat down in a big tub of water, and drank Kool-Aid out of a Pepsi bottle he held between his paws. I was still trying to recuperate when the bear grabbed me and started pulling me back into the ring. He wanted to wrestle some more, but I was like a rag doll as he dragged me around the ring. Then he proceeded to take his tongue and lick me across the face. His tongue was long and rough as it slid across my face time after time. It was disgusting! The owner said the bear seemed to like me. Oh, great! How would I ever get out of the ring? By now, I was too tired to wrestle the bear, and he decided to smell me in embarrassing places. At that, I was up and out of the ring in a flash. It must have been quite a sight, as the whole crowd was laughing hysterically. I'm afraid I was the talk of the shopping center for a while.

I wish I could say that's the end of the bear story, but it's not. We all went back the next day to see how the bear was doing. The owner asked me to wrestle him again—for nothing this time, to draw a crowd. And the bear really liked me. Guess what? Yes, I did it again. Though I was ready for him this time, he was still far too much for me to handle. And he loved licking me. Yuck! And no, I didn't stay in the ring for three minutes—but I gave everyone a good laugh.

When this story hit the college football newsletter, the incoming freshmen couldn't wait to see the guy who wrestled bears in the "off season." So during fall practice, I had a great story to tell. I told it over and over and over, embellishing it a bit more with each telling. I've done some crazy things in my time, but that has to be one of the craziest!

When I wrote to Pat about the episode, she was shocked, but she got a great laugh out of it too. She made the mistake of telling her mom, who was *not* impressed. I'm sure she was thinking, "Who is this weird guy my daughter is dating?" I hadn't met Pat's parents yet, but I'd met her grandparents, and they were okay with the whole thing. They got a big laugh out of the story and were only disappointed that they hadn't seen the event.

It's great to have some really funny memories. I prayed that Pat and I would make many memories together in the years ahead. I couldn't wait for summer to be over. I looked forward to seeing her face when I gave her the engagement ring. I prayed that her dad would be okay with everything, since I knew he wanted us to wait until after graduation. I prayed that God would work it all out.

CHAPTER 4

WEEPING FATHER

Pat has stopped reading and has come over and is rubbing the top of my head. Ahhh, that feels good … don't stop! Oh, there's a noise at the door. It's Stephanie and Haley and Jonathan. I'm so glad to see them. Our little Jonathan is growing up fast, and Haley is becoming a big girl. Look at Jonathan. He reminds me of our other kids when they were small and of our little one who died before we could know it. I wonder what made me think of our baby who died. Maybe it's knowing I'll be reunited with our baby soon. That will be awesome! I remember, it was a difficult time for both of us.

We married in August after our sophomore year. We were lucky enough to get a job as dorm parents for a girls' dorm, where we were given our apartment rent free and were paid monthly. Our salary took care of our food but little more. It was hard to finish college as a married couple, but we were determined to do it. The dorm job was an answer to prayer.

Our junior year was uneventful until spring, when Pat found out that she was pregnant. We were very happy and couldn't wait until December when we'd be parents. We were almost finished with school, and we were planning to work out babysitting arrangements with some friends whose baby was due in November.

It was the end of September, and we were getting a little worried as Pat was not feeling any movement and the doctor hadn't been able to get a heartbeat. We waited another week and then decided to go to Colorado Springs for the weekend and check in with the doctor there. After classes on Friday, we headed to the Springs. On the way, Pat began to bleed and cramp. I was distressed, and I prayed for God to help us get home quickly. When we got there, we called the doctor, and he insisted we meet him at the hospital. After getting Pat checked in, I called our parents and told them what was going on. I stayed by Pat's side as she continued to have severe pains and was bleeding badly. After she was tested, we learned that our baby was dead and had been dead for many weeks. The doctors wanted Pat to continue in labor and deliver the dead baby. I was in shock that she would have to do such a thing. I prayed for God to help her and ease her pain and protect her as she delivered. They made her as comfortable as possible, so I quickly went out to grab a bite to eat.

When I got back, I was stunned. Pat was as white as a ghost. She had an IV in her arm, and medical people were working on her. It scared me, and I thought she was dying. I cried out to God to save her life. I learned that while I was gone, Pat had delivered our dead baby. The realization hit me so hard that I stumbled and almost fell down. I kept asking whether Pat was going to be all right, but no one was answering me as they were all busy working on her. I fell into a chair and cried out to God again. Finally, I was able to see her and talk to her, but she was groggy from the medicine. We cried for our loss and shared our love for each other, and then I let her sleep. I talked to the doctor, who said that Pat had been in grave danger. There was a lot of decay in the afterbirth, and he was afraid that toxins might have gone into her system. At that point they were trying to keep her as comfortable as possible and were watching for signs of infection.

I went back to her room. I sat and watched her as she slept, thanking God for answering my prayer and saving her life. I continued to pray that no infection would set in to cause complications. As I drifted off to sleep, all I could think about was our little baby that we would not see until we got to heaven. I prayed for Jesus to take good care of our little one, who I knew was safe in His arms.

As Pat began to wake up, I went to her bedside. We sobbed and held each other to try to shut out the pain. I prayed with her, but she seemed hard to console. My heart ached for her. I understood that since she had carried our child, she had already bonded with it so that the loss was much harder on her. After a few days she was able to come home, and the doctor believed she would not have any problems with infection.

That was the first heart-wrenching time in our lives, but I was certain that we would face many more over the years. Because the baby had been dead for a while, its sex could not be determined, but we know that we'll recognize our child when we get to heaven. God was there in the midst of that trial, and He was faithful, always faithful.

Chapter 5

Encourager

Oh, look at little Jonathan. He is such a cutie with his red hair. I hope he keeps that red hair. I wish I could see him grow up and that he would know his grandpa. It brings tears to my eyes to think about the things I'll miss seeing: Princess Haley, our only granddaughter; Jonathan, our little redhead; Ethan, our first grandchild and first grandson; Micah, our second grandson; Jonah, our third grandson and the youngest for a while; and my beautiful children: Stephanie and Dan as they eventually have grandchildren of their own, and Clayton and Heidi as they will finally have girls—daughters-in-law. I am going to miss so much, but I know I will be so busy in heaven that I won't even think about it. I am a man truly blessed by God! Thank you, Lord, for my precious family. I remember when we began our own family after graduating from college and heading to Farmington, New Mexico.

After Christmas we began to contemplate our future, especially where we would teach after graduation in June. We sent our applications and went to job interviews. We knew that we didn't want to go back to Colorado Springs right away; we wanted to go somewhere different, somewhere away from home where we'd be on our own. We started praying, or should I say I was praying, as Pat seemed indifferent. I couldn't understand her not wanting to pray, but I left it alone. I really thought she was struggling with her relationship with the Lord, and I needed to pray harder for her to find peace. Ever since our baby died, she had not had much peace or comfort.

We had some good offers from California, but they didn't include coaching, which I felt led to do along with teaching. Finally, a good offer came from two schools in Farmington, New Mexico—Farmington High School for Pat and Hermosa Junior High for me. The Hermosa job included both coaching and teaching, and the pay was good. Farmington was a small city in the four corners area of New Mexico, away from Colorado Springs but not too far. I talked with Pat, and she said she didn't really care what we did, just whatever I felt led by the Lord to do. So we decided to take the jobs.

After spending the summer in Colorado Springs working and raising money to make the move, we loaded a small U-Haul trailer to pull behind our car and headed toward New Mexico, desert land, Navajo territory—all foreign to us. We felt like Abraham and Sarah, picking up and moving to an unknown country. I had made a quick trip down for an interview, but Pat had been interviewed over the telephone.

As soon as we arrived, we looked for housing, and the pickings were slim. We ended up buying a mobile home that we parked in a questionable trailer park. We could actually watch the TVs in the trailers parked on either side of us. That trailer was our very first home, and we fixed it up and settled down in our new city and state.

I felt the need to find a church home right away. In the weeks to follow, we visited several churches. The one we both liked best was the First Baptist Church. We enjoyed the preacher very much and felt right at home in the young adult Sunday school class. A number of our fellow teachers attended there, so we already had friends.

Pat was teaching physical education and coaching gymnastics and swimming at the high school, and I was teaching history and coaching football and basketball at the junior high. We both loved our jobs and loved the new environment, new culture, new places to visit, new friends, and new church. We thought we knew why God had brought us there—but we were yet to realize the real reason.

On the weekends we would take short trips to Navajo Lake, Albuquerque, Santa Fe, the Indian ruins, and so on. We were having a great time exploring new sights and sounds. We both had to travel quite a bit for our coaching jobs, so we'd try to go together whenever we could. By the end of the first year, we'd seen much of New Mexico and were settling well into our new environment.

Everything was great—except for Pat's attitude toward church. Every time we left a service, she would find something wrong to say about the sermon or the Sunday school lesson or something. I felt that her discontent was much deeper than what she was sharing. I began to pray for her to find some peace.

The Lord heard and answered my prayer in an unusual way. Pat and I had volunteered to be counselors for an upcoming citywide revival, and we were attending the training class. As I watched her in class, I saw that she was crying and brushing tears from her cheeks. After class she said she wanted to see our Sunday school teachers, an older couple. I wondered what was wrong. Finally she looked at me and said that she wasn't saved and she was tired of pretending and living a lie and being miserable. I was shocked, but I wanted to help her, so we headed to our teachers' home. Pat burst from the car, ran to meet the wife, fell into her arms, and cried out that she was not saved. The sweet wife stroked her hair and said that she knew it and had been praying for her. I went with the husband into the kitchen, and Pat and the wife sat in the living room.

Pat told me later that this sweet woman shared with her how to have a personal relationship with Jesus and then led her to accept the Lord and become a Christian. Pat said that she'd had only a head knowledge of Christ, and she knew she needed a personal relationship with Him. She literally glowed when she came out of the living room with a huge smile on her face, declaring that she was saved. We drove home rejoicing together in the Lord and praising Him for saving her. We knew then why we had come to Farmington and to that church.

Pat's and my relationship blossomed even more. I didn't think it could get better, but it did. We both grew spiritually in the next two years so that we enjoyed witnessing and sharing our faith with anyone who would listen. I'm glad that I was discerning enough to listen to God as He led us to that place. God was teaching me a lot about obedience and about listening to His voice and following Him no matter what.

The Lord continued to bless us as Pat gave birth to our sweet Stephanie, who was born in Farmington, New Mexico, on April 12, 1970. A few months before Stephanie was born, the Colorado Springs high school from which I'd graduated called me and offered me a teaching job and a position as head football coach for the next school year. Wow, this was a great opportunity! What were we to do? Pray! We both spent many hours praying and seeking God's direction. We loved Farmington, but we wanted to raise our baby near our families and friends. Finally, I felt in my heart that we were to return to Colorado Springs and make our home there. When we moved that August, we knew that it was the right move and that God had a special plan for us in Colorado.

It would be years before we'd see what that plan was, but God brought us there to enable us to grow spiritually and build a firm foundation in Him that would serve us well in His plans for our future. Once again, I was obedient to His calling on our lives, even though in the eyes of other people it didn't make sense.

CHAPTER 6

OBEDIENT SERVANT

It feels good to lie here and think about the early years. The memories are sweet. Ah, here is Pat, and she's talking to me. What is she saying? Oh, yes, she is reading some emails and cards from our friends and family. I'm glad she continues to do that even though I can't respond. I feel so blessed. How precious are our friends, who continue to remember us. That last card was special. It brought tears to my eyes. Please, Pat, wipe my cheeks and my eyes. She must be reading my mind, as she's wiping my eyes and speaking softly to me. I know these days are hard for her, but I also know that God will give her the strength she needs to make it through. I love to feel her touch on my face and to hear her voice. I remember what a young, inexperienced couple we were when we moved back to Colorado. God was faithful to lead us to the right church for our growth.

The move went well. We were able to buy a small house before we arrived, and we had some time to paint and fix things up a little before we moved in. It was our very first house, and we were proud of it. It was good to be back near family and old friends. Unfortunately, I had to begin with football training right away since it was August and the games would begin soon. Pat was great and did most of the unpacking and settling in. It was exciting for me to be the head football coach of the school where I'd graduated years before. Some of the same teachers were still there, and they greeted me and made me feel welcome. I loved teaching history and economics, and I especially loved coaching and working with a great team and staff. I was very glad that God had directed me back to Colorado.

We had prayed and decided that Pat would stay home with Stephanie, and we would learn to live on my teaching and coaching salary alone. It was fun to come home each evening to Pat and Stephanie, to share that day's experiences and to hear about their day as well. I knew that was what family was all about. It was wonderful to sense God's presence in our home and know His guidance for each day.

We found a great church that strengthened our doctrinal foundation as we continued to grow spiritually. We started out in a young married class, but soon we were teaching eleventh and twelfth graders. We loved it! Our students were challenging but lots of fun too. They would come over to our house, where they had fun playing with Stephanie. We became very close to some of the kids and kept in contact with them for many years.

A couple of years later our precious son, Clayton, was born in Colorado Springs. Our little house was getting a bit crowded, but we didn't mind. Pat was still at home and loved being a mother. Stephanie enjoyed being a big sister and took her responsibility very seriously, although she was only two years old.

Football was beginning to demand more and more of my time, leaving me less time for my family. I loved the game, coaching, and my boys, but I loved my family more. I began to pray about what God would have me do. When the answer came, it was a tough one. I needed to resign from coaching and spend more time with my family. I gave my notice for the following year. It was certainly one of the harder decisions in my life, but I have never regretted it. Each afternoon I would have fun playing with the kids and giving Pat a little break. The evenings were Pat's and mine once the kids were in bed and the house was quiet. When I was coaching, I often got home after the kids were in bed, and then I was too tired to talk. I knew I'd made the right decision.

Our little house was getting smaller and smaller as the kids got bigger and bigger, so we began to pray about a larger home. We put our house up for sale, and in almost no time it sold. Where were we going to live? The Lord took care of that: a military family had to leave in a hurry and needed to sell their house, so we got a great deal on a much larger house with a fenced yard and garage. We were thrilled to have all the extra room for the two kids and the dog. Also, the house was only a short walking distance from the school.

Pat and I loved our church, and by then we were teaching college students. Some of the Air Force cadets would be bused in for church, and we had a great ministry to them. Some of them would even spend the weekends with us, and they loved to play with our kids. They said that coming to our house made them not miss home quite as much. We had a great time with that class—taking trips here and there, teaching them God's Word and watching them soak it up. It was truly rewarding for us both. In addition, the students touched the lives of our children.

One thing I've always enjoyed doing is playing jokes on people. I started working during vacations and summers at a toy/hobby store in downtown Colorado Springs. My mom was already working there, so it was fun to be with her. The store had some great costumes and gag gifts, and I had a ball with them.

My favorite time was when I dressed up in a gorilla suit and sat in the store display window as part of a promotion. As people would walk by and look, I'd surprise them by waving. The looks on their faces were priceless, and many would come into the store to check me out. I would stay perfectly still. Sometimes they'd walk up and down the sidewalk outside, checking me out. I had a great time with that outfit. Once when a young boy came into the store and grabbed my fur, I turned around and said, "Stop it, kid." The kid jumped a mile in the air and screamed for his mom. She began to scold him for lying, so I had to save him by talking to her. At other times I would just walk around the store in a weird mask and come up behind people just to see their reaction. I made that store the talk of the city!

One Halloween, I dressed up in a giant bunny suit and went to our associate pastor's house. He answered the door and quickly tried to close it, but I stuck my foot in the door and yelled, "Trick or treat!" The pastor was flabbergasted and kept trying to close the door, but I stood firm in my giant bunny suit. Finally, I gave in and let the pastor know who I was. It was a great prank. I was always playing tricks on Pat and the kids, and they were never sure what I was up to. We had a fun family!

As we were getting comfortable with our lives in Colorado, feeling as if God was going to let us stay there forever, God began to move on my heart to go into full-time Christian work. I wasn't sure what—a pastor, missionary, Christian school teacher, or something else. All I knew is that God was speaking to me, and I couldn't refuse. I was worried about telling Pat, but finally we had a quiet evening to ourselves, and we talked. To my amazement, God had already been impressing upon her heart that we needed to move and begin a new ministry of some kind, and she was worried about how to tell me. We laughed together and praised the Lord for this confirmation, and we began to pray diligently about the move. It would not be easy, but we had to be obedient.

By now I was assistant principal/athletic director. When I talked with my senior administrator, he was startled. When I met with the board, they did everything to talk me out of leaving. But I gave a strong testimony, explaining that I had to be obedient to the Lord. At the end of that year, I gave them my resignation.

Those in our church family were sorry to see us leave after more than nine years with them, but they were excited about our plans. I chose to be ordained as a minister at our church before we left. God was leading us to Memphis and to Mid-America Seminary. I prayed that God would give me some answers about our future while we were there. Our move would bring quite a change since I had never been that far east in my life. The kids were a little hesitant at first because they didn't want to leave their school, their grandparents, and everything familiar. We sat down as a family and talked about the move and why we were going, and then we prayed about it. At last we were all in agreement, and the kids were actually excited.

Our house sold quickly—in fact, on the very day the realtors came to look at it. We needed a place to rent before we left. The house across the street from my folks was empty, and the owners agreed to rent it to us. It was good to be close to the kids' grandparents before leaving, and we were able to spend a lot of quality time with them.

We felt like Abraham and Sarah again, heading into the unknown but following the Lord's leading. What did God have for us in Memphis? What would our future hold? What was it that God wanted me to do? I turned these questions over and over in my mind. All I knew was that we were to move to Memphis and that I was to go to seminary. God would give us direction from there. It was scary but rewarding to be obedient to God's call to the unknown.

CHAPTER 7

DEDICATED EDUCATOR

Oh, Lord, the days are so long and drawn out. When will this end? I look at Pat and the family. They are very tired and sad, but they try not to let me see. I feel responsible for their agony, though I know I am not. It was the accident. I fought hard at Shepherd to get well enough to use a wheelchair and move on with my life, but it wasn't to be. I hate to have others take care of me ... but I can do nothing for myself. Lord, keep my spirits up and my eyes on you—and on all my wonderful memories.

It was August 1979 when we made our move to Memphis, and it was like stepping out into the unknown. I had never been farther east than the western side of Arkansas, and now I was actually crossing the Mississippi River. This was going to be quite an adventure for all of us. Before we left Colorado, I had accepted a job at a church in West Memphis, Arkansas, just across the river from Memphis, Tennessee. As the church's bus pastor, I would be in charge of several buses that went out every Sunday morning and brought people, mostly children, to the church for the children's service. The church would allow me to work around my seminary schedule, so it seemed an ideal job. And I had been nervous about my lack of job security!

We found a small house to rent, and Pat went to work at the high school as a teachers' aide since she didn't have an Arkansas teacher's certificate. Things seemed to be moving along smoothly. Pat and I, the kids, and several teenagers who worked with us went out each Saturday morning and visited neighborhoods in the city to invite children to church. Pat and two teenagers who helped her had their own bus route in a trailer park, so we spent a lot of time visiting there and encouraging children to come to church. Soon we had more than fifty coming each Sunday, and the other bus routes began to grow as well. The work was exciting, especially seeing the joy in the faces of the children as we walked through the trailer park and talked with them. Many Sundays we would have to go into some of the trailers to find clothes for the children to wear, and often there were no parents in sight. The children wanted to come to church so badly that we couldn't turn them away. Pat would sing songs with them as we made our way to church. It was a happy time!

The children's church was our responsibility as well. Each week Pat worked the puppets with some teenagers she'd trained, and I presented a children's message. We did a lot of singing, but the puppets were the highlight of the service. The children could earn "bus bucks" by coming each week, and more "bus bucks" if they learned the memory verses. Pat and her group put together a puppet show for the children's Christmas party. At the party the children could use their "bus bucks" and buy gifts for their parents, friends, or themselves from the many donated items. We were thrilled to watch the joy and excitement of the children as they selected that perfect gift. It was a special evening for all of us!

Seminary was going well, but it had been a long time since I'd had to study so intensely. I'd made up my mind before going that I would not study while our kids were up but would spend time with them and study after they went to bed. At first I thought it wouldn't work because I had so much work to do at home. But God was faithful and allowed me to get it all done after spending time with Pat and the kids. I've never regretted my decision. I watched too many seminary students study hard and lose their families, and I vowed that would not happen to us. God also blessed me with good grades as I was obedient to Him.

After Christmas, things at the church were not going well, and we began to pray about whether we'd made the wrong decision in taking the job just to have security. We sought counsel from our pastor in Colorado Springs, and he shared his wisdom with us as we continued to pray. Finally, I knew we had to leave the church. My heart was heavy, as we had grown to love "our kids" in the bus church. It was an extremely hard decision, but I knew I had to obey the Lord and move to Memphis without a job for either me or Pat. Talk about a scary time—we were truly stepping out in faith! With what money we had, we moved into a rented townhouse, and by taking money from our savings, we enrolled the kids in a Christian school. I had visited the school before. The church that owned it had a huge bus ministry, and I'd already learned a lot about running one. When we visited the church, we knew it was where the Lord wanted us to serve.

Pat was able to get a job in the kitchen at the seminary, and I took whatever preaching jobs I could get. The kitchen job did not work out. Pat tried hard to get other work but was always overqualified. We finally decided the Lord wanted her home to help the kids with their schoolwork and to support them by being there in the afternoons. Don't ask me how we made it through, as I don't know. All I know is that God met every need. We never went hungry or without clothing, and we paid all our expenses. Many people from our home church sent us money from time to time to help us get by. For the first time in our lives, we were totally dependent on the Lord and not on ourselves. It was a very freeing experience, and I now know how that time of trusting was to serve us later on.

One event that stood out during that first year was what we call the "shoe miracle." One night at the dinner table, Pat shared how badly the kids needed shoes, as they had outgrown the ones they had. I said we should take our request to the Lord and that He would supply our needs. Stephanie asked whether she could be specific about a particular kind of shoe, and I said, "Of course you can." It was a great lesson for the kids in trusting the Lord. It was also a great lesson for us in trusting God to answer the kids' prayers. After dinner we prayed specifically for the shoes and waited for God's answer. The next day when the kids came home from school, Pat was holding a check for sixty-five dollars that had come in the mail that morning. She said that God had sent the check even before we prayed, and that now the children could have their shoes. They were jumping up and down, excited to think that God had heard and answered their prayers. Also, it was good to know that He'd sent the money even before we voiced the need. It was a great lesson for all of us: God will supply our needs; He is faithful all the time.

That year was a hard one, but 1980 was beginning to look better. It was around springtime that year when the church approached me about coming to the school, Southern Baptist Educational Center

(SBEC), as the high school principal. The school's leaders had heard about my background as an administrator, and they needed one for the rest of 1980 as well as the next year. I felt torn about leaving the seminary, so I began to pray. I sought counsel from Dr. Gray Allison, then the head of Mid-America Seminary. After his wise counsel and through much prayer, I agreed to take the position at the end of the school year so that I could complete at least a year of seminary. I wrestled hard with the decision, but I felt that God had brought us to Memphis for this very reason—to get me involved with Christian education. The year at seminary was a bonus. Again I knew I wanted to be obedient to the Lord and His leading.

That summer as I was on the new job and preparing for the next school year, I realized that the school needed a part-time home economics teacher. That was not Pat's teaching field, but I knew she could do the job well. She agreed to take it since it was part-time and would allow her plenty of time with the children. That year, she fell in love with the job and eventually got certified in home economics. The job turned into a full-time position.

The years at SBEC in Memphis were some of the best years of our lives. The children thrived and loved the school, Pat was enjoying teaching again, and I felt that I was right where God wanted me and my family to be. We grew spiritually at the church, we made many new and lasting friends, and our hearts became passionate about Christian education. In our years at SBEC, we saw it working in the lives of our own children. We saw the evidence of loving, caring teachers as well as a God-centered curriculum.

Pat and I had the opportunity to start a Christian cheerleading camp at SBEC. Soon the idea spread, and other camps were formed around the Southeast. Pat was our cheerleading coach, but she was also helpful in making these camps a ministry for the Lord. It was exciting to be associated with a school and a church that had God's vision planted firmly in everything they did. It was a privilege for us to serve the Lord for those years at SBEC.

In 1984, the new ACSI (Association of Christian Schools International) director for the Southeast Region approached me about coming on staff with him as the student activities director. I was overwhelmed that he had considered me for the job. I met with our headmaster. He was not happy about the possibility of my leaving, but he told me he'd pray with me about it. Pat and I prayed and prayed. (After all, accepting this position would mean another move, and Stephanie would just be starting her junior year.) The director wanted me to work part-time for two years, traveling back and forth to Atlanta when necessary and working over the phone. We would be moving in June 1986, which didn't seem far away at all. We agonized over this decision: What does the Lord want us to do? Then God spoke to my heart and gave me clear direction that we were to move. As I shared with my family, I could see that the kids had mixed emotions. It was hard for them because they loved the school and had made many friends, but they knew that again we had to be obedient to the Lord. As I accepted the position, I knew that God had given me the right direction for the future.

Those first two part-time years were hard as I was trying to run the high school and go back and forth to Atlanta for ACSI. But the Lord saw me through, and finally in June 1986 we moved to Atlanta. What most people saw as a crazy move—a lower salary for both me and Pat, and no help with tuition for the kids' schooling—we saw as another opportunity for God to prove Himself true to us and through us. We found a good school for the kids, and Pat worked at ACSI as my secretary until she found a teaching job. Once again, as we let the Lord have our lives, He moved us where He wanted us to live and gave us the work He wanted us to do. We were excited about the future in Atlanta.

CHAPTER 8

MISSIONARY HEART

Oh, what time is it? What day is it? I see Pat sitting quietly in the chair across the room. Her eyes are closed. Is she asleep or praying? Her lips are moving, so she must be praying. Wait, she's singing. I hear the music in the distance, and she is singing along with it. I love the soothing and comforting music she has on. I hope she'll come over and sing to me—I love to hear her sing. She must have read my thoughts as she is coming to the head of the bed. Now she is looking down at me and singing and touching my face and rubbing my head. How I love her! I see her love for me in her eyes, but I also see tears. Please don't cry, Pat, I'll be all right. Actually, I'm looking forward to heaven. You've been reading a book to me about heaven, and it makes me want to go there. It won't be long now. I loved our time in Atlanta. The Lord did such wonderful things while we were there; we have great memories.

---◆---

Atlanta! Who would have thought we'd be calling Atlanta home? It was great having Pat in the office with me. We had only four staff members in the office in 1986—the director, his secretary, me as assistant director, and Pat as my secretary. It was hard with such a small staff, but it was also a lot of fun. The office did not have a printer, so we jokingly said our printer was down the street at Quick Print. Once a day one of us would make a trip to "our printer" and make whatever copies we needed. Also, we had no computers in the office, but we had the finest memory typewriters, so we were well equipped. It's amazing how we got by with so little, but we did.

The Southeast Region was growing, and both the director and I had to travel a lot. It was exciting to see the growth. We started with a total of perhaps fifty activities, and that number has more than tripled. We enjoyed spending quality time with the administrators when we visited the schools. We could visit them all as there were fewer schools then. I'm grateful for the growth, but the early years were special to me. I could really see God at work in our schools and in ACSI as well. The conventions and conferences also began to grow, and we had to find bigger and bigger facilities. It was an exciting time to be a part of ACSI and the Southeast Region.

Pat and I rented a house during that time. We didn't have the money to buy one since we were paying tuition for Stephanie and Clayton. Although she was in her junior year, Stephanie adapted well, and Clayton has always been able to fit in anywhere. We were happy, and God was blessing our family and our ministry with ACSI. The church we attended was just what we needed, and we settled in and began to serve the Lord there. I taught a young marrieds class with Pat by my side to help out and to keep everyone informed and involved. We were always a team wherever we ministered. God was using us, and it was rewarding.

Four years later we were able to buy a house out in the country, in Loganville, and it was great to have our own place at last. Stephanie was in college then, and Clayton had just finished high school. It was a lovely country home with a yard that I could "sink my teeth into." I loved having a yard, and I worked hard to make ours beautiful.

For two years we drove the distance to our church, but then God spoke to our hearts about attending the small country church in Loganville. We joined, and we loved the people and the pastor. Over the years we watched that church grow and blossom into a thriving ministry for the Lord. God continued to use us to teach young married couples and minister to their needs. Again, we were happy and comfortable with our life. But God was ready to shake us up a little, and we weren't quite prepared for what He had in store for us.

The Co-Mission Russian projects started around 1992, when Russia opened its doors to the Western world. The Southeast director had gone on one of the trips, and his experience stirred a great deal of interest in me. The Co-Mission trips had been created to educate the teachers and administrators in the school districts in Russia. The

Russian minister of education had asked if groups could be sent over to teach Russian teachers how to bring the Bible back into their schools after seventy-five years of absence. It was a wonderful opportunity to reach out to the Russian people, to share with them the Bible and biblical integration.

I had a strong desire to go, but Pat was firmly against it. She didn't understand how I could want to minister to our "enemy," for that was what she'd been taught about the Russians. I continued to pray, and in November 1992 I was asked to make a trip. Pat really fought me about it, constantly bringing up reasons for me not to go. But I knew in my heart that God wanted me to go, and so I had to go. I had to obey God's calling on my life. I prayed with Pat, and I told her I had to go and I needed her blessing. She finally agreed, but she was fearful that I'd be killed or captured and would never return. I had to raise my own support for the trip, and she secretly hoped I wouldn't raise enough to go.

On the Sunday before I left, we had a special singer at the church. He sang a song that spoke to her heart and broke it, about whether we'd "laid it all down on Mount Moriah." God would not leave her alone until she laid me and this trip on the altar. She gave me her blessing for the trip, and I was overjoyed to know she was behind me in what lay ahead. I knew that God was going to do something wonderful and that I'd share the experience with Pat and we'd rejoice together.

It was hard to say goodbye to my family as I left on the day after Thanksgiving, but I knew that God was leading me to Russia. The amazing thing was that, as a history major in college, I'd taken Russian history and had always wanted to visit Russia but knew it was impossible at the time. God works in mysterious ways. I had studied the history of the country that I was about to visit. As I boarded the plane, I was so excited that I couldn't sleep. When we arrived in St. Petersburg, I couldn't keep my eyes off the beautiful buildings and the people walking about the streets. I was actually in Russia! I felt as if I had to pinch myself to believe it.

We stayed all night in St. Petersburg, and the next day we boarded a small Russian plane to fly to Petrozavodsk. When we landed there, we had to unload our own luggage and then ride to the terminal in the back of an open truck. Remember, it was winter in Russia, and it was cold! Our bags came down through an open chute, and we grabbed them as quickly as we could, making sure we had everything. Then we loaded them onto an old bus that would take us to the hotel and the conference center.

The conference was awesome. The small group of administrators I taught were friendly and eager to learn. My translator was a young teacher who spoke wonderful English. She wanted to know everything about my family and about America. Just like us, the Russian people had heard only the propaganda the government wanted them to hear. The only thing they knew about America was what they'd heard and seen on TV and radio. We found out quickly that we are all alike, with the same fears, hurts, desires, and dreams. I kept hearing the same words over and over: "You are just like us." And it was good to hear that. I didn't want them to think I considered myself better because I was an American. The week went by much too quickly, and we had to say goodbye and go on to another city.

As we got to the airport for our flight to Pskov, we wondered why we were staying on the bus. Then the pilot got on the bus and explained that we couldn't fly then because a huge fog had come in around Pskov and the plane wouldn't be able to land. We knew that we had to leave soon because our time in Pskov would be short and the conference was planned for the next few days. After we got off the bus, we lifted our petition to the Lord. Our leader led everyone in praying, singing, and reading Scripture. That was the best prayer meeting I'd attended in some time, right there on the frigid tarmac at that airport in Russia. We were in the midst of cold weather and a frustrating situation, but it was thrilling for us to sing and praise the Lord.

Finally, the pilot came to the bus and said that the fog had lifted and we could fly. We all shouted "Amen" in unison. The airport at Pskov would be closed by the time we landed, but some lights would be left on so that our plane could land. This news made us all feel more secure as we loaded our luggage and flew to Pskov. Right after we landed, we watched the fog roll back over the airport. What a sight! It was like the parting of the Red Sea. A Russian set-up man came to our leader and said he wanted to know this God whom even the weather obeyed. He got saved that night; it was terrific!

Right away we learned that the conference was in jeopardy as a Russian Orthodox priest was trying to stop our teaching. Our leader met with him and then showed him the Jesus film in the Russian language. He wept through the whole showing. Then he agreed to have the conference, but he wanted to sit in on all the sessions. At the end of the conference, he addressed the teachers with tears streaming down his face. He said that the conference was the greatest thing he'd ever been a part of, and he blessed our work. We spent another wonderful week there, working with the teachers and making friends. It was exciting to watch the teachers as we taught them Bible stories that they'd never heard and explained how they could relate each story to their students' lives. As Bibles were passed out, many of the teachers grabbed one, hugged it to their heart, and exclaimed, "I have only dreamed of owning my own Bible." In the United States, most of us have several Bibles in our homes that we don't even use or read. But that was the very first Bible most of the teachers and administrators had ever owned.

That Co-Mission trip truly changed my life. I will never look at missions the same way again. Also, I'll never look at my Bible the same way again, and I'll never take it for granted.

God did a work in my heart for missions on that trip. I've never gotten over it, and I pray that I never will. God opened my eyes to His world, especially His love for people everywhere and His desire to see them come to know Him personally. I had many opportunities to share my faith on the trip, and I know that we planted many seeds among those Russian people. I pray that someone else will do the watering and that those people will come to a personal relationship with Christ. God sent me with His message of love and forgiveness, and I came away filled with His love for the Russian people.

When we returned to the United States, it was great to see Pat and the family. I'd missed them a lot and couldn't wait to tell them all about the trip and the miracles God performed right before our eyes. They were eager to hear everything, and I watched their eyes as I shared the stories. I especially saw a tenderness for the Russian people begin in Pat, and I began to pray that she would soon go to Russia with me.

The Lord blessed! He opened the door for me to make two more trips to Russia, this time with Pat. We made a trip in August 1993 to

Krasnoyarsk and Norilsk in Siberia. Again, the Lord worked mightily among the team, and we had a wonderful time with the teachers and administrators in those cities.

In December 1994, we made a third trip to Russia. This time we were up near the White Sea at Kotlas and Novodvinsk, where it was very frigid! This time the team was much smaller, but we had a glorious time meeting the convention delegates in those areas. We were up past the Arctic Circle, so we had "black nights"; there were only a few brief hours of very dim light. But even though it was dark, God was moving in the hearts of the people, and we had a tremendous ministry experience as we taught them how to integrate the Bible into their lessons.

My mission experience was not limited to Russia. Many years later, I made two trips to Haiti under the supervision of a very good friend from Canada. These were unforgettable trips, as I saw the poverty and the horrible living conditions of the people there. But they always smiled and radiated the love of the Lord. It made me appreciate all the more what I have in the United States. Teaching these Haitian Christians was sheer joy, and I came back a changed man after being with those sweet, caring people.

All these trips had a major effect on my life. They opened my eyes, more than ever before, to the world. It truly is God's wonderful world, and He loves all the people unconditionally. I think these trips to Haiti and to Russia stirred my love for missions. God began to soften my heart for the world and to show me what He planned for me in the future. I never dreamed I would sell everything and go to the mission field. But when God is in our lives, miracles happen!

CHAPTER 9

CALLED TO MISSIONS

As I think about the past, it is amazing how the Lord prepared me for the mission field. As I lie here in this bed all alone in my room, I have time to remember those wonderful times in Russia and Haiti. I'm so thankful to the Lord for such great memories. I only wish I had time to make many more. As I glance around the room, I see pictures of my family. Oh, I love my family! I'll never forget when Ethan, our first grandson, was born. What a thrill it was to hold him in my arms for the first time. Each grandchild after that has added joy upon joy. O Lord, I am a man so very blessed! Dear God, I thank you for all the precious treasures that you have given me—my wife, my children, my grandchildren, my friends, and on and on. Lord, one thing I will always thank you for is our call to serve in Hungary. Those were some of the best months of my life, and I will cherish the memories forever.

It was in the fall of 1996 that I became the Southeast regional director for ACSI, and the region was growing so fast that we had to hire additional staff. It was an exciting time for Christian schools in the United States and especially in the Southeast. I was highly honored to be a part of this growing movement, and I felt that this would be my calling until I retired. However, again the Lord had other plans for me and Pat.

The European director invited Pat and me to come to Budapest, Hungary, for the administrator conference for Poland, the Czech Republic, and Slovakia in February 2004. I was thrilled to be invited and was looking forward to speaking to the administrators and seeing some of Hungary. I had no idea what God had in store for me!

The office staff was wonderful to us when we arrived, and immediately we felt right at home. Our hosts gave us a quick tour of Budapest, and we saw the lights of the city at night. It was a breathtaking sight! Budapest is one of the most beautiful cities I have ever seen. The next day we were able to go downtown for some shopping and sightseeing. I was impressed with the long history and the ancient traditions that surrounded me as I walked down the streets. I was saddened when I heard of the oppression that the people had been under for so many years. It was a joy to see the monuments declaring their liberation. My heart was stirred as I looked around. Budapest is a great city, and Hungary a brave, wonderful country.

The conference was going well, and the administrators had given me a very warm reception. They were eager to hear what I had to share, and they asked many questions afterward. Pat was getting involved as well, and she seemed to be enjoying herself. We made many new friends and spent our mealtimes encouraging these precious folks to keep on doing their best in the midst of difficult circumstances.

During one of my sessions, as the translator was relaying my message, I know that God spoke loudly and clearly to my heart. He said, "This is where you and Pat are to serve me." I was so taken aback that I almost lost my train of thought with the translator. After the session I went upstairs, thinking, "How am I going to tell Pat about this message from the Lord?" Upon entering the room, I noticed that she had been crying. She said that she did not want to go home; she loved this country and these people, and she wanted to stay and work. I couldn't believe my ears! God had spoken to her and prepared her for what I was going to share. Amazing! I related my encounter with the Lord, and we hugged each other and praised Him! Who were we to be given the honor of ministering to these wonderful people? As I led us in prayer, we thanked God for clarifying His call on our lives and trusting us with this new ministry.

We said nothing to anyone, as we wanted to continue to pray and confirm that we had heard the Lord correctly. We prayed as we flew home, and we prayed earnestly after we arrived. Finally, we called the ACSI International Office and spoke with the staff there about the possibility of our moving to Hungary. They were in shock and were thrilled to have us help with the European staff. Then we had to share our decision with our children. I knew it would be difficult to tell them. We are a very close family, and our decision to go that far away was not going to be popular. They were shocked at first, but as we talked about it, they began to warm up to the idea—not thrilled, just resigned.

Then we began to think of all the things that needed to be done. We had to raise a very large amount of support money, sell our house, sell our cars, sell our furniture, find a mission sending agency, get a visa—all in a year. It seemed impossible, but our God is a God of the impossible. The staff in Budapest were excited, and they said they'd start looking for an apartment for us. It was amazing to see how God moved quickly through each of these apparent obstacles.

God miraculously provided the funds for printing our support letters and the postage for mailing them out. Then a woman came to our condo and asked whether we wanted to sell it anytime soon. Our visas were completed in record time, and we found a great sending agency from Canada. Things were happening very quickly, and I jokingly said, "At our age things have to happen fast." By now we were very excited about the move and were busy planning what to take and what not to take. Because our condo had sold so quickly, we had to spend six months living with our daughter. But those special months gave us wonderful opportunities for interaction with our children and grandchildren.

In June we attended the Pre-Field Orientation (PFO) for Janz Team, our Canadian sending agency in Winnipeg, where we had a great time building friendships that would last a lifetime. We learned a lot about cultural adjustment and what emotions to expect on the field. PFO was a valuable experience!

Later in July we participated in the PFO that ACSI held in New York, and there we continued to build on the lessons we'd learned in Canada. More emphasis was put on adjusting to the culture and not being the "ugly American." We were joining their culture and must not push our culture on them. Again we learned a great deal, and both PFOs were valuable to our quick adjustment when we arrived in Hungary.

Finally, the day arrived, August 8, 2005. We were at the airport with ten pieces of luggage, and we were headed to Budapest. The check-in went smoothly, but the goodbyes with our family were very difficult. As Pat and I headed to the gate, we were in awe that God had done all of this in just a little over a year. We were sixty years old and beginning a new ministry in a new country—and we couldn't wait to begin. We thanked the Lord for the wonderful honor of serving Him in this new way.

CHAPTER 10

THE MISSIONARY

It must be raining outside, as I hear the rain beating against the window. I'm facing away from the window, so I can't see anything but the door. I think it's still very early in the morning; it's hard to tell as the hours all run together. The time goes slowly at night and in the early morning hours. The nurses and techs are kind and considerate, constantly checking on me to make sure I'm all right. I feel much weaker today, and in my heart I feel it won't be long before I go to be with my Lord and Savior. I can't wait to run and hug Jesus and to bow at His feet in adoration and praise. I will be leaving this crippled old body behind and will have a new glorified body—praise the Lord! I can't wait! I know it is hard for Pat and the kids to let me go, but I must go. I know God will take good care of them. God took such good care of us when we arrived in Hungary and in the wonderful months that we ministered there. What a blessing those nine months were to me and Pat! I thank you, Lord, for even that short time on the mission field.

The plane was flying low over the beautiful city of Budapest, our new home, and it was an awesome sight. As the pilot circled over the incredible old bridges that spanned the tranquil Danube River, I had to pinch myself to realize that this was real and that we were beginning our lives on the mission field in Europe. Moments later we landed and, after collecting our ten pieces of luggage, emerged to find Alan and Malinda Brown (the ACSI Europe director and his wife) and Laci (the Hungarian coordinator) waiting for us with huge smiles and a bouquet of flowers for Pat. After many hugs and sighs of relief, we loaded the luggage into two vans and headed to the ACSI office for lunch. We were home! We were missionaries in Europe! Who would have ever believed this a year ago?

We had a warm greeting from the rest of the staff at the ACSI office. Then we settled into our apartment over the office, which would be our temporary home. Anna, the office secretary and conference coordinator, had been working diligently to find us an apartment and had one for us to look at. We rested the remainder of the day and visited with the staff. The next morning we went to see our apartment possibility with Anna. We met Alexander, the owner of the home. He spoke no English, so we were glad Anna was with us. We would be renting the top floor of a house less than a mile from the office. It resembled an alpine cabin, with wood floors and a beautiful wood ceiling that was slanted like one in an attic. It was immaculate, and that really impressed us. It had two small bedrooms, a living room with an area for a desk and computer, as well as a very small kitchen, bathroom, and toilet room. The only drawback was the stairs we'd have to take, but other than that, we loved it. We decided to take the apartment. The owner gave us a great price, but we'd have to wait a few days while the cleaning was completed. We felt a bond with the owner, who was kind and pleasant to us. Later we met his wife, Eva. The couple would become our very good friends over the next nine months.

We had few belongings with us—our clothes, a few kitchen utensils Pat felt she couldn't live without, some food items we wouldn't be able to get in Budapest, and three boxes of books we'd sent ahead. We had no furniture, so shopping was high on the agenda. When Laci and his wife, Rita, took us shopping, we had our first experience with IKEA, the wonderfully huge European store that sells everything—and I mean everything! We were grateful to have Laci with us, as we often needed translation help. After that first day, we were supplied with beds, dressers, a sofa, a chair, a desk, rugs, and a few other necessary items. It was quite an event! Our purchases would be delivered, and the set-up guy would come the next day to put them all together. It was a learning experience, but fun. Our home was taking shape.

Adjusting to money matters was tough. The exchange rate would change from day to day, so I kept a close eye on it. I would take out money when the exchange rate was good, and I'd try not to draw it out when the rate was not so good. We paid all our bills with cash, so there was no need for a checking account. Our U.S. bank had allowed us a larger withdrawal from the ATM each day, so the ATM served as our bank. Thus there was a definite change in the way we took care of our money, and it was challenging, to say the least.

Money was not the only issue; dealing with the language was the toughest challenge. Going to the store for groceries became a two-to-three-hour event because we had to try to distinguish what we were buying through the pictures or the few words that Anna had given us to use. The language was always a huge barrier when we had questions about anything or needed to find out what we owed for our purchases. At times it was comical, but other times it was very frustrating. I soon learned how to count, and that helped a lot. Then I began to learn essential phrases like "I am hungry" (always necessary), "How much?" "Where is the toilet?" and "Where am I?" I soon mastered the fine art of ordering hamburgers at McDonald's, and that accomplishment made me feel proud! But soon we knew that we needed expert help, so we hired a tutor, a sweet young lady from our church. She began working with us three times a week when we were in town. We loved learning, but it was a hard language.

Pat and I loved the Hungarian people and their country. We felt an immediate bond with them that was hard to explain. It was as if we were meant to go there and minister, as if God had been preparing us all our lives for this very ministry. I felt like a little boy in a candy shop with money to purchase all the candy I wanted. I felt so blessed that God had honored us with this vital trust of ministering to the educators in Europe; I prayed that He would give us the power to do the task. I could think of no better way to spend my last years in education than ministering to those who have such a strong desire to learn. I prayed, "God, may we be up to the job you have for us!"

We hit the ground running! We spent a few weeks getting acquainted with the public transportation system and learning how to get from here to there, and then we were ready to work. The first big event would be the International Student Leadership Conference, held in Budapest at the end of September. There would be about 250 students and sponsors from national and international schools all over Europe. All the delegates would have to speak and understand English.

This was a much anticipated event for the office and for us. Alan brought a speaker from the United States to minister in the general sessions, and in addition we had a number of workshop sessions for the participants to choose from. I would be doing a session on purity with the guys, and Pat would do a purity session with the girls. Still other sessions would be going on at the same time. We were excited and ready to get started!

The conference was a huge success. The speaker challenged all of us, and it was fun to get acquainted with the teachers and students. Many students made commitments to stand strong for the Lord in their schools when they returned. I was impressed with their deep desire to serve the Lord with all their heart, regardless of the consequences. I believe we made some lifetime friends. That conference began our ministry in Europe with a bang! God was allowing us to see His world and to feel His heart for it.

Our next big challenge came in October as Laci, Pat, and I went into Ukraine for a teacher workshop. It was held in a town just over the border from Hungary. This trip was our first experience of crossing the border into another country, and the crossing was quite interesting. We stood in a huge line and underwent a number of inspections, as smuggling had been taking place between the two countries. The town was not far once we crossed the border. The host director and his staff were genuinely kind to us and made us feel welcome. Laci and I led sessions that evening, and then we were taken to the school. It was a boarding school, where we had dinner and were given our sleeping arrangements. We had our own room, but it had twenty bunk beds. We had our pick, as the students were on vacation. It was fun to feel as if I were back in a dorm setting. It was hard to sleep. I was exhausted, but I was also excited about tomorrow's sessions.

The next day was even better than the evening had been. The teachers were eager to learn, and they asked many questions. I had to adjust to working through a translator, but Laci and I made a great team. Pat sang for us, and even though the words were in English, the song was well received and seemed to minister to everyone. My heart broke as I heard from one teacher after another of the hardships under which they taught. Many didn't have a textbook for every child, and some didn't have chalk, writing tools, or paper for the children. But the amazing thing was that they were dedicated to teaching their children about the love of Jesus while they taught the academic courses, with or without teaching tools. They always had a smile on their face as they spoke of their love for teaching in a Christian school. I was deeply humbled by their commitment and obedience to the Lord. I knew that I would never be the same after spending time with these very special servants of God. As I said goodbye to everyone, I was looking forward to the day when I could come back and minister to them again. I hoped it would be soon.

It took us a while to get over that moving experience with the Hungarians in Ukraine, but we didn't have long to wait for our next assignment. In November we headed out for ten days in Romania. We would cross the border without a translator, but we'd meet our translator just over the border in Oradea. Needless to say, I was a little nervous about crossing into Romania without a translator, but I trusted God to work it all out. He did, and it was a smooth crossing with a border guard who spoke English. God was definitely in control.

After we'd met our translator in Oradea, we spent the night at a Christian college. In the morning we spoke to the students at one of the Christian schools. Next, we drove to Sibiu in the southern part of Romania, stopping along the way to stay overnight at a lovely retreat center. In Sibiu we stayed at another retreat center, and I spoke at the Christian school and held an after-school workshop for the teachers.

From Sibiu we drove north into the Carpathian Mountains to the city of Sucheva. We had a delightful experience there, staying with a sweet family that lived across the street from the school. They welcomed us warmly and treated us as special guests in the three days we were there. We spoke to the students during the day and enjoyed observing some classes. That evening I held a workshop for the school's teachers and other invited teachers in the area.

The next day we visited a boarding school for orphaned Gypsy children. The school, which was run by the Mennonite church, was considering joining ACSI. I shared with them what ACSI was and how membership would benefit them. The school was amazing! It had wonderful facilities, including its own dairy cows, an auto mechanics shop, a carpentry shop, a cooking school, and a sewing school along with the usual academics. We were quite impressed with what the school offered its students and how well the facilities and grounds were kept. We had a wonderful visit with the elders and the directors of the school.

Later that day, one of the directors took us on a little sightseeing tour to visit some unique villages where black pottery was made. We also toured another monastery, an extremely old one. It was beautiful, and we wanted to stay longer, but it began to snow. As we headed back, the snow became heavier and heavier, and I began to worry about traveling home the next day.

It snowed all through the night, and it was still snowing when we woke up. I was nervous about driving that big van through the mountains on the snowy roads. But we prayed and asked God to protect us, as we couldn't stay any longer. When we left early on Sunday morning, God cleared the way—again, just as He had parted the Red Sea—and we faced hardly any traffic as we made our way over the mountains. Once we were out of the mountains, the roads were less snowy, and the traffic began to pick up. We were thanking and praising God all the way.

We stopped to eat dinner after getting through the mountains. I think we all began to relax a little, even though driving the Romanian roads takes quite a bit of skill. I continually dodged horses and carts, and I also had to be on the lookout for people. They tended to walk on the roads, since there was no shoulder. But the Romanian countryside is beautiful, and the people are warm and caring.

I'll never forget our trip through Romania, even though it had its thrilling moments. After dropping off our translator in Oradea, we smoothly crossed the border into Hungary. I will have to admit that it was good to be back where I knew where I was going.

In December, we returned to the United States for a visit with family, friends, and supporters. It was wonderful to see my children and grandchildren. I finally got to hold my new grandson, who was named after me. We made many great memories during our stay that Christmas. It was a wonderful time, but I missed Hungary and all our friends there. I couldn't wait to get back.

In January, we returned to Hungary and began preparing for the director conferences to be held in February. The first conference, which was for the Hungarian directors, was in Budapest, followed by a conference for the Polish, Czech, and Slovak directors a week later, also in Budapest. I was the speaker for the Hungarian conference, and God really spoke through me. We had a great conference! All the staff shared in speaking at the other conference, which was very well received by all the directors. What a joy to share with these dedicated directors, who work so hard and have so many struggles. The prayer time was my favorite time, as they all share their praises from the past year and their needs for the year to come. It was encouraging to see them praying for each other and ministering to one another. It was uplifting for me to witness these sweet saints of God. Each one will always have a special place in my heart.

The Romanian director conference was a few weeks later in Gyula, Hungary. Gyula is near the Romanian border, close enough for the Romanians to come and enjoy the restfulness of its beautiful hotel and hot pools. We had a special speaker from the United States as well as a separate speaker for the early childhood directors. There was a large attendance, and everyone seemed to enjoy all the sessions and evening workshops. Again, I was overwhelmed by the spirit of these directors as they continued forging ahead with determination. I was amazed at how much they could do with so little. They taught me a lot about commitment and total surrender.

Through these conferences, I saw God's hand moving over Europe and using these dedicated directors and their staff to spread the gospel. The children are finding a personal relationship with Jesus, and they are leading their parents to find the same relationship. God is truly using Christian schools to evangelize that part of the world. We are honored that God allowed us to witness this movement in Europe.

April and May were basically planning months, and I spent many days visiting schools and leading one-day workshops. Laci and I were busy traveling all over Hungary, visiting one school after another and holding afternoon sessions. Pat was having some problems with her hip, so she couldn't travel with me very often. She spent most of her time resting her hip. There were many sights we wanted to visit, but we would have to wait until she could walk better. We spent our time talking and driving around Budapest. We finally were able to purchase a car, thanks to our wonderful supporters, who sent special offerings for our car fund. It was a small car, an Opel, but it ran well and scooted us down the road. Pat had to relearn how to drive a car with a stick shift, and she did quite well. We were grateful to have this additional convenience, especially for going back and forth to church.

Our time in Hungary was flying by, and we were enjoying it immensely. Now we were at the nine-month mark. We could hardly believe it. The summer looked as if it were going to be great with a number of teacher conferences, and we were planning to take some time off to visit another country. We had plans, but God had other plans—plans that we were not prepared for.

CHAPTER 11

COURAGEOUS HERO

As I lie here in the quiet of the morning, I think of what marvelous months we had in Hungary! What a special blessing God gave me for my remaining months on earth! I told Pat some time ago that if I had known before we left for Hungary that I would soon die, I would have gone anyway. That time was one of the best in my life. It's hard to explain, but to know that God was using me to touch the nations was awesome. The apostle Paul knew that he would die as he went to Rome, and he went anyway; that is the way I felt. What better time to meet the Lord than while one is serving Him in obedience.

I am getting tired now, and I feel life slipping from me. I hope Pat gets here soon. Oh, I hear her talking to someone in the hall. I'm glad she's here. Now she's talking to me and telling me about the emails and cards. I hope she'll read some Scripture to me, as it strengthens me so much. Yes, she's going to do just that. Sometimes I think she can read my mind. Maybe that's what happens when you are married for forty-one years. Oh, I love to hear God's Word. I wish I could say thank you, honey—but I think she sees it in my eyes. She says they are giving me a new mattress that will help with the pressure sores. They will be moving me soon. Ugh! I dread that, as I know it will start my choking again.

Here they come to move me. Lord, please help this to be a smooth move. I am so big that it takes several people, even though I have lost over thirty pounds. Ugh, ooh, hurry and get it over with. Oh no, I can't breathe! Someone help me! I'm choking again. Help me! Pat is right here helping me breathe, and they are using the ambu bag to force air into my lungs. It's helping, but I am still struggling. Oh, God, please don't let me die struggling like this. Pat is beginning to pray in my ear, and she prays that very thing. We talked several weeks ago, and I told her I didn't want to die struggling to breathe but to go peacefully. She is praying for the Lord to ease my breathing—and He does. I'm beginning to breathe better. Now I am much better. Thank you, Lord. Pat is touching my face and head, and she's trying to soothe me. I love her so much! I wonder if she knows that I am drifting away.

I think she senses it, and she only wants me to be comfortable. How did I get to this point? I don't remember too much about the accident in Hungary, but Pat has filled me in with some details. It was the day after Mother's Day and I had to speak at a nearby school.

———◆———

It seems like only yesterday when I was traveling back from Nagykorus after a wonderful conference with the teachers. Anna had been with me to translate, and I was driving. We were discussing the events of the afternoon when I noticed the traffic slowing for an accident ahead. I began to slow down when I heard Anna gasp. Then there was a noise like a giant explosion, and the van was catapulted off the road into a ravine. The next thing I remember is Anna holding my hand and asking me if I'm all right. The back of my seat had broken, and I was lying flat on my back. I told Anna I had no feeling in my arms or legs. She kept telling me to lie perfectly still, that the ambulance was on the way. I think I blacked out again, as the next thing I remember is being in the hospital room with several Hungarian nurses and doctors surrounding the bed. I couldn't understand them, and that was frustrating. Several of them tried to speak a little English, and all I could make out is that I was in serious condition and they were waiting for my wife's permission to do surgery on my neck, which was broken.

Hours passed. Pat still had not arrived, and I was drifting in and out of consciousness. Finally, I saw her approach the bed, and she looked very anxious and worried. She told me my neck was broken; a chip had broken off one vertebra and was pushing against my spinal cord, causing the paralysis. The chip had to be removed to reduce the pressure, and a rod and screws had to be inserted to secure the remaining fractured vertebrae. Tears were running down her face, but she asked me what I wanted her to do. I immediately said to do the surgery, as I didn't see any other choice, and to pray for God's guidance for the surgeon. After she left, I was prepped for surgery.

Several days later, I regained consciousness, and Pat was standing over me. She was smiling, but I could see worry on her face. She shared with me that the surgery had gone well, and everyone was praying for the paralysis to subside. I could barely talk, but I whispered my love for the Lord for sparing my life and my love for Pat—and then I was gone again.

Most of the first week, I was sedated heavily. Eventually I had to have a vent tube inserted to ease my breathing. Clayton arrived to help out that Saturday, and he kept encouraging me to fight on. I was determined to fight to live and to walk and to move my arms again. The Lord and I had many hours together as I poured out my heart to Him, asking Him to save my life and let me go home to see my family. Discouragement came for me when the doctor had to insert a tracheotomy tube to help me breathe. The procedure felt so permanent that I had to face the fact that I might always be on a ventilator. Part of me wanted to give up, but I knew I had to keep fighting and struggling to live. Evidently, God had a plan in all of this, and I had to wait on Him.

The accident was not the first time that Pat and I had persevered together. In 1998, Pat had been diagnosed with breast cancer, and we had not been sure of the prognosis. But we pulled together as a team and fought back the urge to give up. Working together—with her fighting for her health and me encouraging her to keep going—was what got us through those months of treatment and recovery. Now, we were facing another "giant," and we would fight and beat this one as well.

Finally, after two weeks in a Hungarian hospital, I was air evacuated to the United States, where I entered Shepherd Center in Atlanta. Stephanie had made all the arrangements, so when we landed, an ambulance took me straight to the center. I was in the intensive care unit for two weeks while the doctors stabilized me and prepared me to be moved to a room where I would begin physical therapy. Before I moved to the room, I was already sitting up in a wheelchair and beginning to eat some solid food. I couldn't wait to get rid of the feeding tube. I had severe pain in my shoulders and neck, the only areas where I had any feeling at all. The doctors finally gave me some medicine to reduce the pain without putting me to sleep.

Once again I was going to fight, and I was going to make it out of that hospital even if it was in a wheelchair. I cried out to God to use me from my wheelchair. My biggest fear was not to be used for the Lord again. I knew that I had to work hard at physical therapy no matter how much it hurt or how dizzy I got. I pushed myself to do the very best I could. After three months, I was using my straw "puffer" to move my wheelchair, I was eating solid foods, and I was off the ventilator except at night. I had worked hard to come that far, and I praised the Lord for my improvement. My best times were when I shared Jesus with anyone who came into the room—nurses, cleaning ladies, doctors, just about everyone.

The day came to go home—to the little apartment that our church had remodeled for us. Stephanie and Dan had an unfinished basement, and our congregation had taken it upon themselves to remodel it completely into a handicapped apartment. When I was wheeled into the apartment for the first time, I could not believe it. It was beautiful, and I couldn't help crying. That apartment was to be our home from now on. How great to be surrounded by our kids and grandkids and to feel such love. It was worth the fight and the pain to get to this point.

Unfortunately, I was home only eight days when I developed pneumonia and had to go to the hospital. I became discouraged again when I was put back on the ventilator and a feeding tube was inserted. I felt as if I were going backward; it was hard to keep fighting. Pat was my cheerleader. She kept encouraging me to keep fighting, saying that I would be back home in no time. I spent three weeks in the ICU fighting to live. There were times when I was not sure I was going to live through the day. But I fought on.

After three weeks, I was moved to an acute care hospital, where I could get more intensive care around the clock. Again, the doctors tried to wean me off the ventilator, but each time I would have to have it put back on. I tried to eat food again, but that didn't work either, so the feeding tube stayed. Eventually, I had to have a stomach tube inserted so there'd be less irritation to my nose. I kept getting pneumonia time and again. Even though I was on a huge regimen of antibiotics, nothing was working. But I kept my spirits up and continued to fight on. I knew that in all of this, God had a plan for me. Again, I witnessed to everyone who entered my room, and I tried to be gracious to all the workers. I praised the Lord, as everyone was kind to me and treated me well.

Two months later, the doctors recommended to Pat that I be moved to a hospice facility, as there was nothing more they could do for me. When she shared this with me, we both cried and knew that the end was near. Part of me wanted to keep fighting to live, so I never gave up even as my body was giving out. The move to the hospice was hard, as I kept having choking spells, but I made it there safely. Pat had decorated the room for Christmas, and it looked beautiful. I wondered how long I would be there before the Lord took me home. I talked and witnessed to the nurses and cleaning ladies, and I joked around with them. After a few days, because of the choking, I had to have heavier sedation, so I was not awake most of the time. Pat continued to talk to me and read to me, and there were times when I heard her. I could feel my body getting weaker and knew my strength was giving out, but I continued to will to live.

<hr>

Here I am lying here thinking about my week in hospice care. Just this afternoon I had a serious choking spell, and I didn't think I was going to be able to breathe again. Pat leaned over my head and told me not to panic and to try to breathe deeply and relax. Finally, after what seemed like hours, I am resting and no longer choking. Thank you, Lord, for peace. Pat has slipped out for a bite to eat, and I know she senses that the time for me to go home is very near. I feel it too, and I am so ready to meet my Lord. I can't describe the wonderful peace that is coming over me, and I am no longer struggling to breathe. I see Pat and the children coming back into the room. It must be late at night as it is dark outside. They all gather around me. They are singing and praying and telling me how much they each love me. Pat strokes my face and head, and she says how much she loves me and how thankful she is for our forty-one years. Then they each kiss me and say goodbye, and I see tears in their eyes.

Please don't cry, as I am going where I can walk and run and hug Jesus. Please be happy for me. I don't think I'm giving up; I'm just giving myself over to Him. I'm going home. What glorious peace to take my last breath on earth and my first breath in my heavenly home! Thank you, Lord, for my life. I pray that it was well-pleasing to you.

FROM PAT

My precious beloved husband, a devoted father and grandfather, went to be with the Lord on Monday, December 11, 2006, at 3:30 A.M. The Lord honored his request and took him peacefully. He simply breathed slower and slower until he took his last breath here on earth. What a wonderful homegoing for a faithful servant of the Lord!

> "I have fought the good fight, I have finished the race,
> I have kept the faith."
>
> 2 Timothy 4:7

> "His master replied, 'Well done, good and faithful servant!'"
>
> Matthew 25:21

> "Precious in the sight of the Lord is the death of his saints."
>
> Psalm 116:15

Thomas A. McClure

I was privileged to be raised in a Christian home. My parents hosted a Bible study for the children in the neighborhood, and through that study I made a decision when I was eight years old to accept Jesus Christ as my Savior. During my childhood my parents and my church did little discipling to help me understand the decision I had made. I was always involved in church activities, but I never really came to the point of developing my relationship with Christ.

Over the years, there were several times when I questioned that relationship, but I was told not to worry because of the decision I'd made as an eight-year-old. This answer would satisfy me for a while, but the question would continue to bother me until after I had married, graduated from college, started my teaching career, had children, gone to seminary, and begun working for the Association of Christian Schools International. Every time I talked to others about my doubts, especially my parents, they would try to persuade me that everything was fine. How could it be otherwise? After all, I was serving as a deacon in the church, teaching Sunday school, and working for a Christian organization.

Finally, on April 5, 1985, I wanted to put all doubts about my salvation to rest. When we came home from church that day, I gathered the family and shared with them the questions that were hindering my walk with the Lord. I decided not to let my pride or my family's pride stand in the way of doing what I'd known years ago I needed to do. That day I shared my doubts with them and prayed to accept Jesus Christ as my Savior. I have never doubted my salvation since. I made the decision public in the church we attended, and I was baptized. As I've shared this story with others over the years, I've found that many people have had similar experiences.

I may have been saved when I was younger, but I did not want my doubts to hinder me, my family, or my relationship with the Lord. My experience has given me a passion for children, for helping them understand who they are in Christ and how they can be used in His kingdom.

I thought I was a Christian for many years, and I did many good things for my family and for others. But until I had nailed down the issue of my salvation, I never understood the peace a relationship with Christ can bring. Once I knew I was a Christian and no longer just thought so, the strength, joy, and peace I experienced were amazing. The issues I'd faced before were still there, but how different they looked through a sure relationship with Christ!

I am very thankful for my parents and for the way they raised me. If I had not had the foundation they gave me, I'd never have made the decision I did later in life. What I've been through has given me the passion I have for people to come to know Christ and to understand who they are and how they can be used in the kingdom of God.

Tom McClure International Teacher Awards

Are you ready to join an exciting new project? As you know, Tom was passionate about missions and education, and he had a heart for helping teachers who make the sacrifice to teach around the world. As we carry on his legacy, join us by donating to the Tom McClure International Teacher Awards to provide grant awards for these dedicated teachers. From our years in ministry, Tom and I realized how helpful it is for people to have funds available for family expenses as they embrace God's calling.

How does the project work? Teachers or administrators who are answering God's call to serve a year or more in Christian international or MK schools overseas and who must raise their own support may apply for an annual award. As a family, we have set up a foundation that will help us give a monetary award, or awards, to selected applicants. The number of awards may vary from year to year, depending on the availability of funds and the number of applicants.

Would you like to donate to the Tom McClure International Teacher Awards fund? Simply write to the address below and ask for information regarding donating to the fund, and we will send you a donor form. All donations are tax deductible.

Would you like to apply for an award from the Tom McClure International Teacher Awards fund? Simply write to the address below to request an application, and we will send you one right away.

Write to   The McClure Family
            343 Courtney Lane
            Locust Grove, Georgia 30248

Help us carry on Tom's legacy for years to come. Pray about giving to help teachers, and pray about teaching internationally. Our family's desire is to honor Christ, through the Tom McClure International Teacher Awards and through everything we do.

Warmly,
Pat McClure

The Tom McClure International Teacher Awards fund, MCP#7545, is a Ministry Charity Project of WaterStone Support Foundation Inc., TID#84-1430063. All contributions are irrevocable gifts under the direction and control of the WaterStone Board of Directors, but the funds will be restricted for the general purposes of the Ministry Charity Project. Information is available from WaterStone, 2925 Professional Place, Suite 201, Colorado Springs, Colorado 80904-8136.